AF575445

Chinese Modern Engineering

SKYSCRAPERS

Edited by Xia Rui Written by Xue Liwei Illustrated by Wang Futing

It’s summer vacation now. Dongdong’s father takes him to Shanghai and visits the Jin Mao Tower.

“What a huge building! It looks like it’s reaching into the clouds!”

“You are right. That’s why we call these super tall buildings skyscrapers.”

Skyscraper

These are also called high-rise buildings. Historically, a skyscraper meant 10 to 20-story-buildings. But now, a skyscraper is usually more than 40 or 50 stories. In China, this term refers to buildings with a height of over 328 feet.

Dongdong and his father get on the sightseeing elevator. The construction outside the window is getting smaller and smaller . . .

"Dad, look. The people and cars in the street are as small as ants!"

"That's because we are standing very high. Do you know, Dongdong, that this building is 1,379 feet high? That's 240 times my height!"

Skyscrapers are not just tall.
They are big, too.

An 88-story skyscraper can accommodate all residents in 70 regular apartment buildings.

How are these gigantic skyscrapers built?

Let's first play a game of "house of cards."

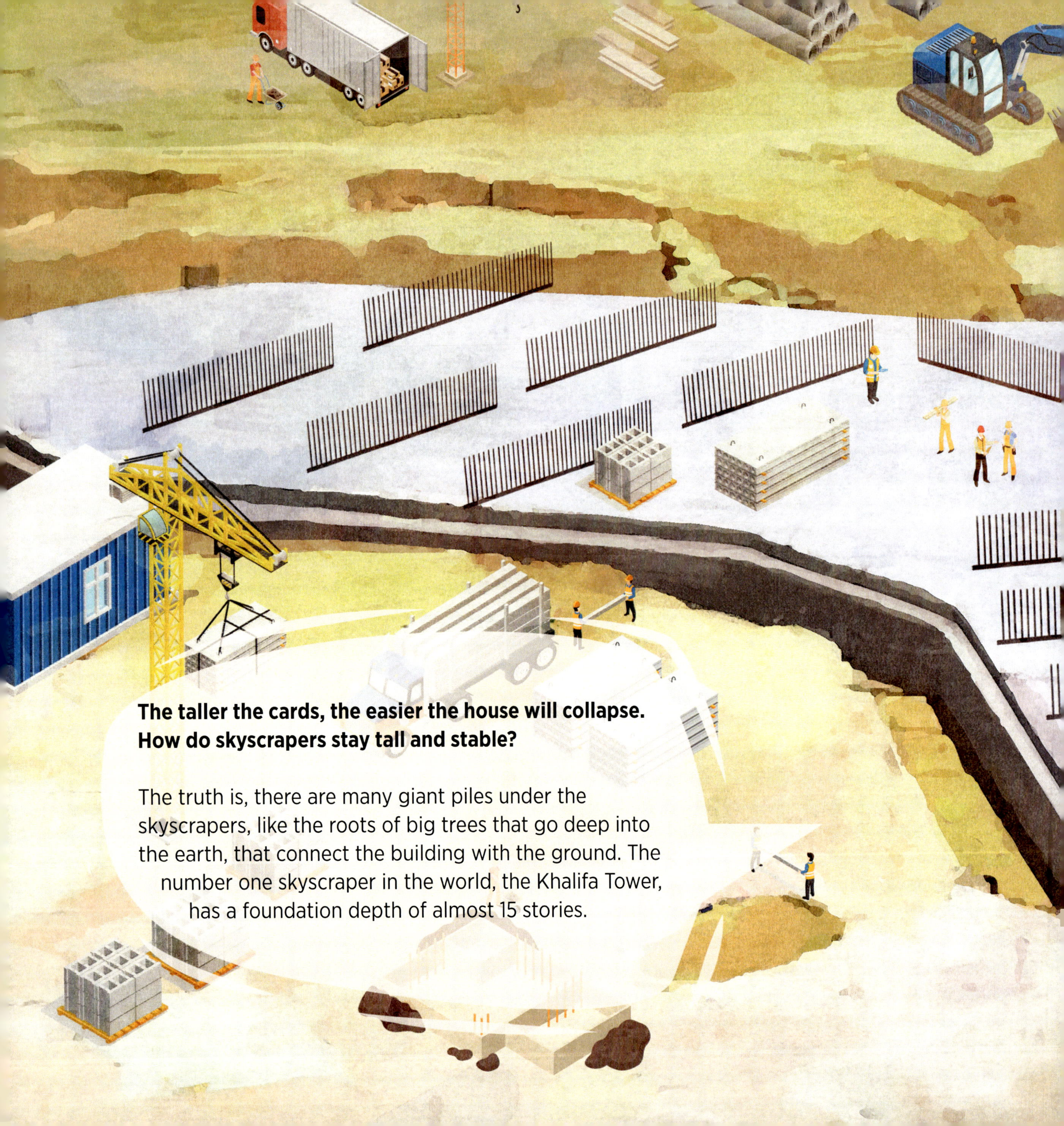

The taller the cards, the easier the house will collapse. How do skyscrapers stay tall and stable?

The truth is, there are many giant piles under the skyscrapers, like the roots of big trees that go deep into the earth, that connect the building with the ground. The number one skyscraper in the world, the Khalifa Tower, has a foundation depth of almost 15 stories.

The reinforcement mat (mesh structure composed of steel beams and columns)
The construction of each floor of a skyscraper consumes hundreds of tons of steel.

Now that the skyscraper has a stable foundation, how do workers make it tall?

The answer is with a reinforcement mat, which is like a steel armor that protects the inner structures of skyscrapers and makes them tall and strong.

The world's fastest elevator is in Shanghai Tower. Its maximum speed is 67 feet per second, which allows it to reach the 119th floor within 55 seconds. It was listed in *The Guinness World Records* in December 2016.

The skyscrapers are so tall. It will take forever to climb the stairs. What should we do?

We can take the elevators to quickly get to the floors we want. It's like taking the skyscraper subway.

We can't live without water. How do skyscrapers provide water?

Workers divide the skyscrapers into sections based on height and place a tank in each section. They use booster pumps in the lower sections to pump water into the tanks in the higher sections. The water will then flow into pipes in each floor for people to use.

When there's strong wind, the big trees will shake back and forth. How do the skyscrapers maintain stability?

This is because of the "stabilizing magic ball" —shock absorbers. The turbulence of the building caused by strong winds will be passed to the shock absorber through sensors, and the shock absorbers will move the opposite direction and reduce the shaking of the building.

Taipei 101 has the biggest shock absorber in the world. Its weight is that of 132 elephants combined.

In stormy weather, big trees are often hit by lightning. This is also very dangerous for skyscrapers.

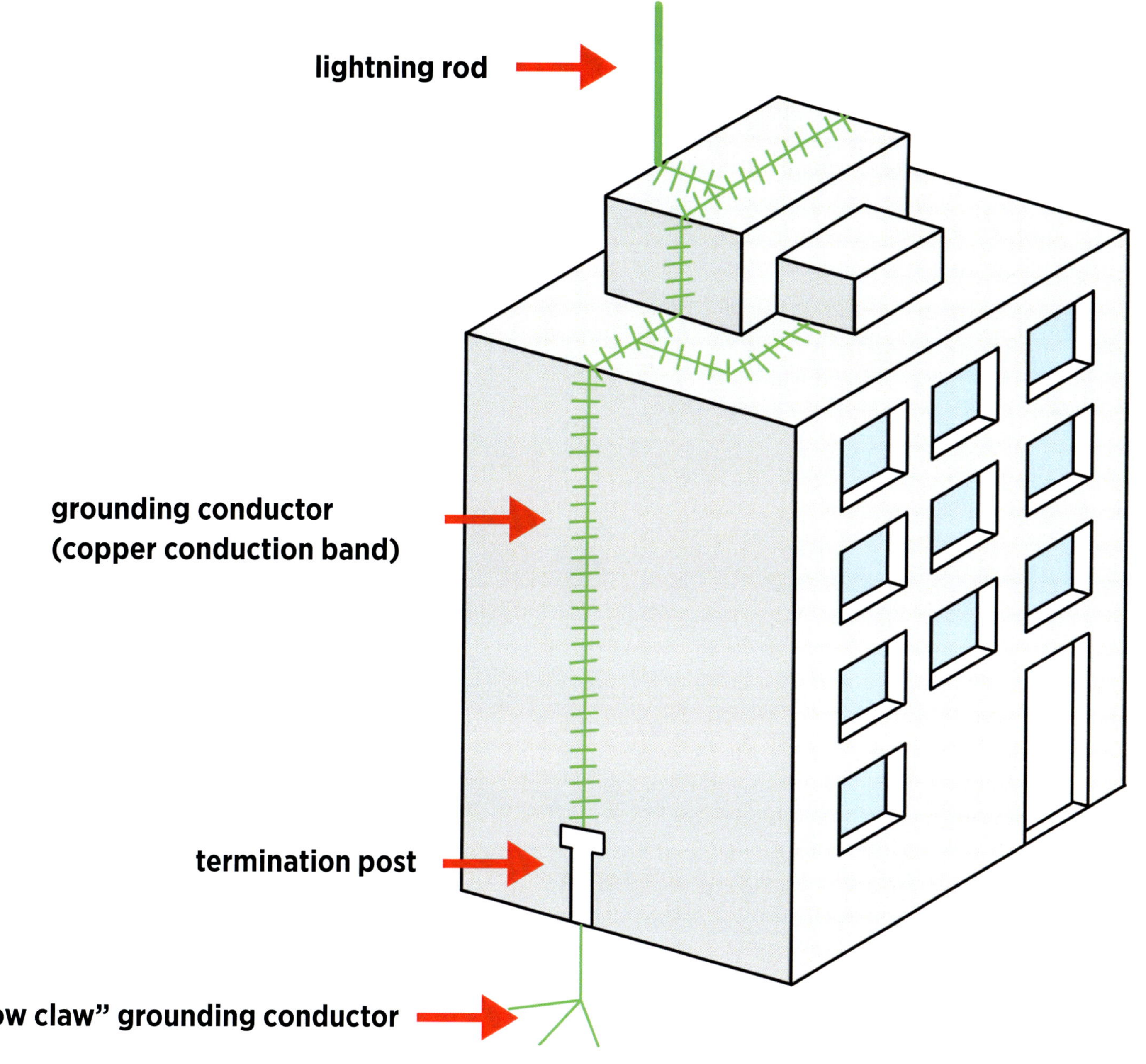

The lightning rod invented by Benjamin Franklin can effectively protect skyscrapers in storms by directing lightning near the building to the ground.

Now we know what skyscrapers are. But how was the world's first skyscraper built?

In October 1871, a serious fire almost destroyed the whole city of Chicago. Ninety thousand people were made homeless.

That was the incident that gave birth to the first metal framed skyscraper made of steel and concrete instead of wood.

Nowadays, there are more and more skyscrapers in the world, and they are growing taller and taller ... So, let's get to know some of the famous ones.

1. Khalifa Tower

Key info:

Ranking: world's tallest building
Height: 2,716 feet, 162 floors
Location: Dubai, UAE

Super elevator—57.4 ft/sec
The world's highest outdoor observation deck— "At The Top" on the 124th floor
The world's highest swimming pool—886 feet from ground, on the 76th floor

In order to prevent the impact of high-altitude strong winds on the tower, the Khalifa Tower is designed based on the structure of spider orchid petal and stem, with connections between its side wings and central core. The six-core structure ensures that the tower is stable enough.

2. Petronas Twin Towers

Key info:

Ranking: world's tallest twin towers
Height: 1,483 feet, 88 floors above ground
Location: Kuala Lumpur, Malaysia

Skybridge

The skybridge connects and stabilizes the two buildings on the 41st and 42nd floors. At about 558 feet above the ground, this 192-foot-long floating corridor is the highest footbridge.

3. Empire State Building

Key info:

Height: 1,250 feet, 102 floors. 1,456 feet after an antenna was added in 1951
Title: one of the Seven Wonders of the Modern World
Location: New York, USA

The film *King Kong* was released on March 2, 1933. In it, the giant gorilla climbs onto the roof of the Empire State Building—which made the best advertisement for it.

Additional fact:

The Seven Wonders of the Modern World are the seven greatest engineering accomplishments of the 20th century chosen by American Society of Civil Engineers.

These are the Channel Tunnel between the UK and France, the CN Tower in Canada, the Empire State Building and the Golden Gate Bridge in the US, the Itaipú Dam between Brazil and Paraguay, the Delta and Zuiderzee Works (a system of dams and dikes) in the Netherlands, and the Panama Canal in Panama.

HOW MANY SKYSCRAPERS ARE THERE IN CHINA?

Ten tallest buildings in the world (2020)

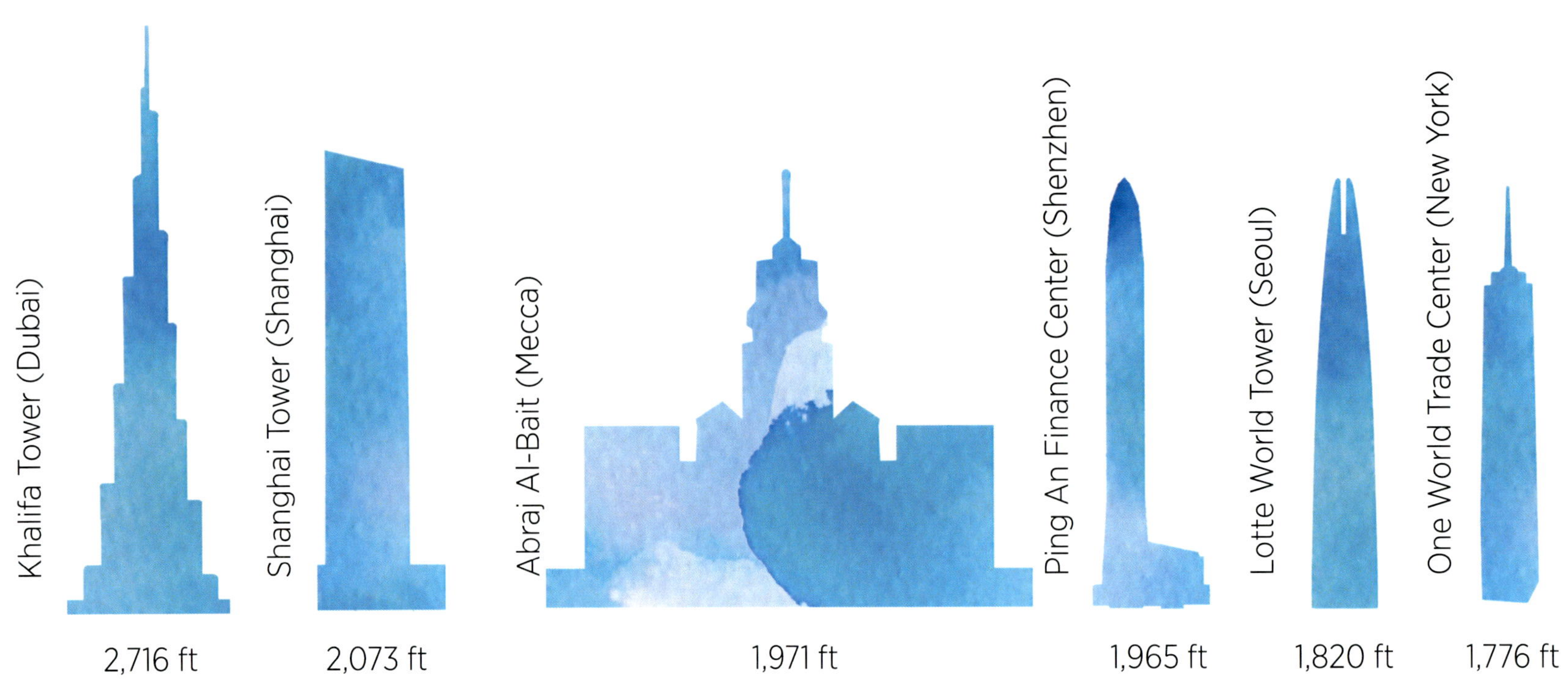

Finished skyscrapers (above 984 feet) by May 2014

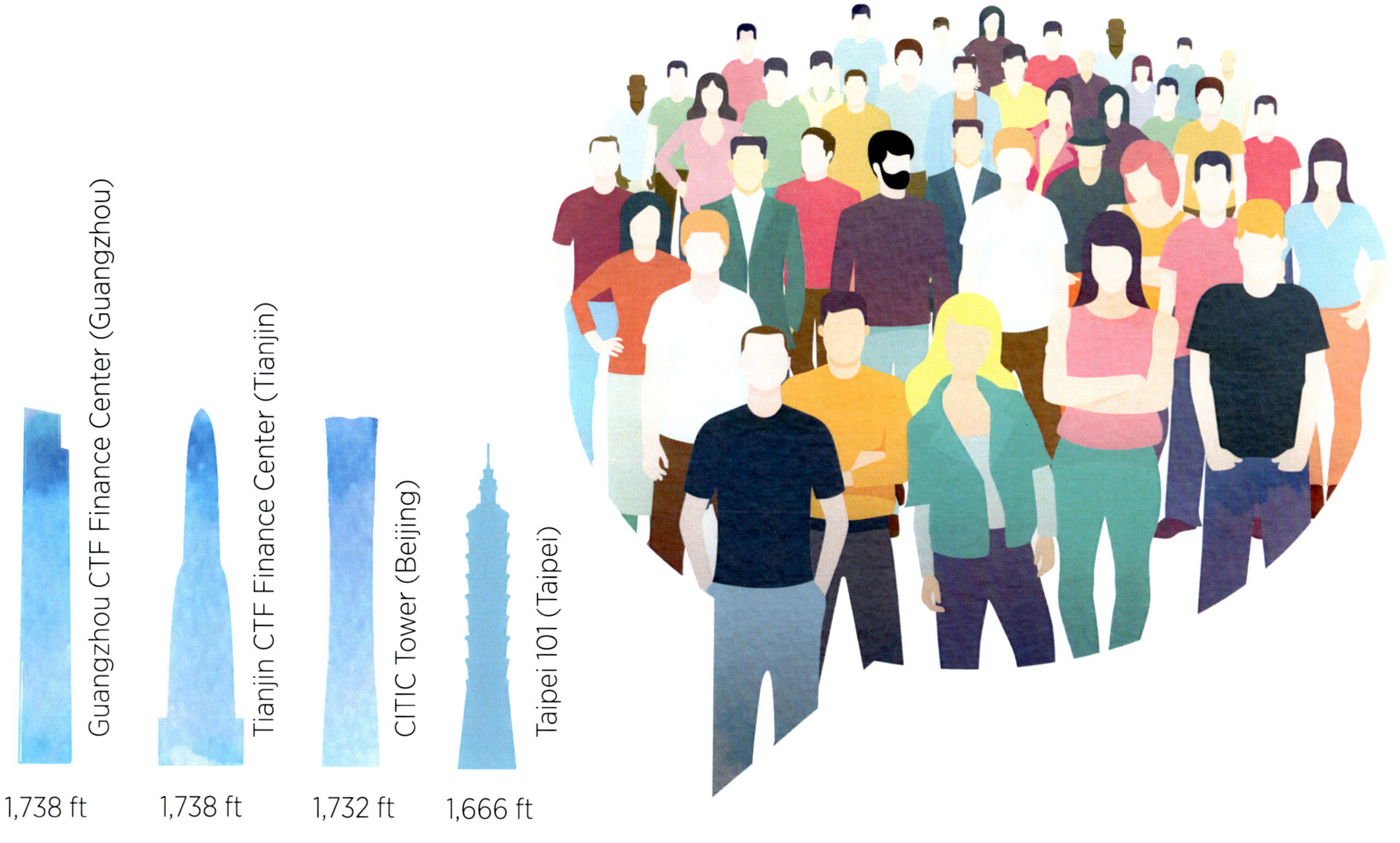

The US had the most skyscrapers in the world for a long time. But in recent years, in China the process of economic development and urbanization has rapidly improved. As more modern metropolises with dense populations and advanced industry emerge, more and higher skyscrapers are now built in China.

Half of the world's top 10 skyscrapers are in China, and 34 of the world's top 100 skyscrapers are in China. Especially Hong Kong, Shanghai, Shenzhen, Guangzhou, and Chongqing are famous for all kinds of skyscrapers.

Hong Kong International Trade Center

Height: 1,588 feet
Ranking: tallest building in Hong Kong

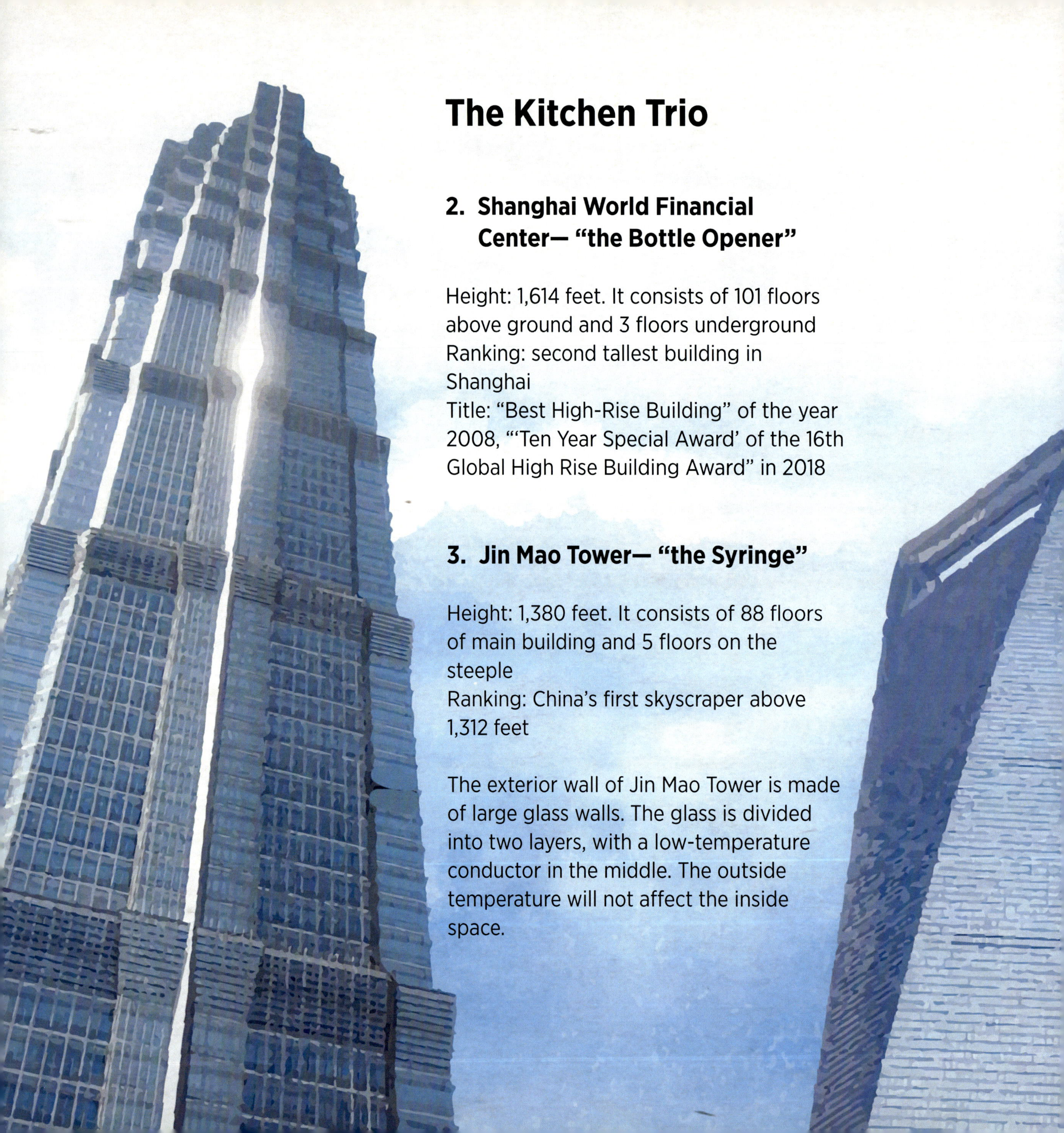

The Kitchen Trio

2. Shanghai World Financial Center— "the Bottle Opener"

Height: 1,614 feet. It consists of 101 floors above ground and 3 floors underground
Ranking: second tallest building in Shanghai
Title: "Best High-Rise Building" of the year 2008, "'Ten Year Special Award' of the 16th Global High Rise Building Award" in 2018

3. Jin Mao Tower— "the Syringe"

Height: 1,380 feet. It consists of 88 floors of main building and 5 floors on the steeple
Ranking: China's first skyscraper above 1,312 feet

The exterior wall of Jin Mao Tower is made of large glass walls. The glass is divided into two layers, with a low-temperature conductor in the middle. The outside temperature will not affect the inside space.

1. Shanghai Tower— "the Whisk"

Height: 2,073 feet (structural height is 1,903 feet). It consists of 121 floors of main building, five podium floors, and five basement floors
Ranking: tallest building in China

The Shanghai Tower has an upward spiral appearance. The spiral starts from the bottom of the building and continues all the way up to the top. As the height increases, each floor is twisted by nearly 1 degree. This kind of design can delay wind flow, which is very important, for Shanghai buildings are often tested by typhoons.

Raffles City Chongqing

Height: 1,163 feet
Ranking: tallest building in Chongqing

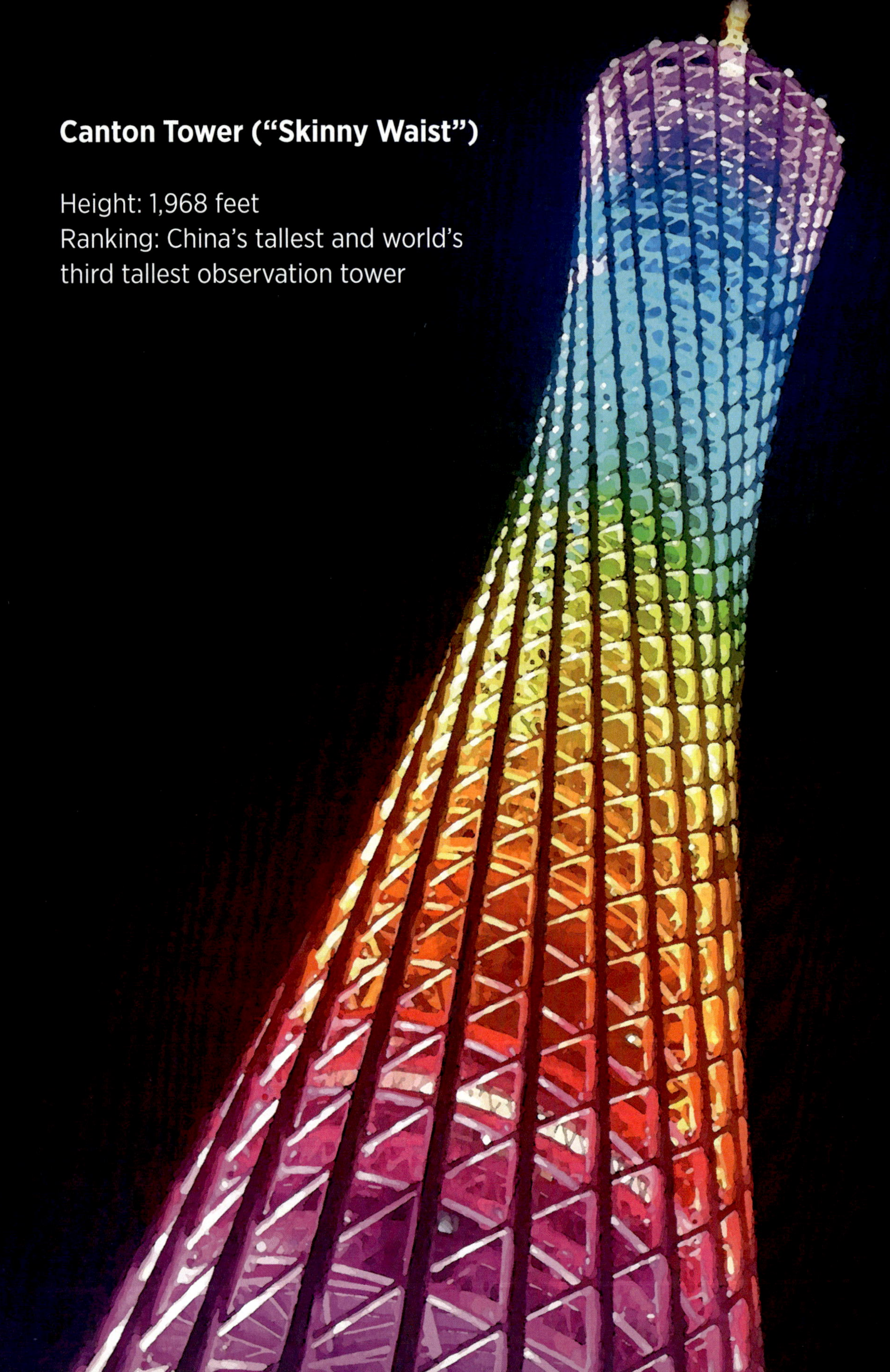

Canton Tower ("Skinny Waist")

Height: 1,968 feet
Ranking: China's tallest and world's third tallest observation tower

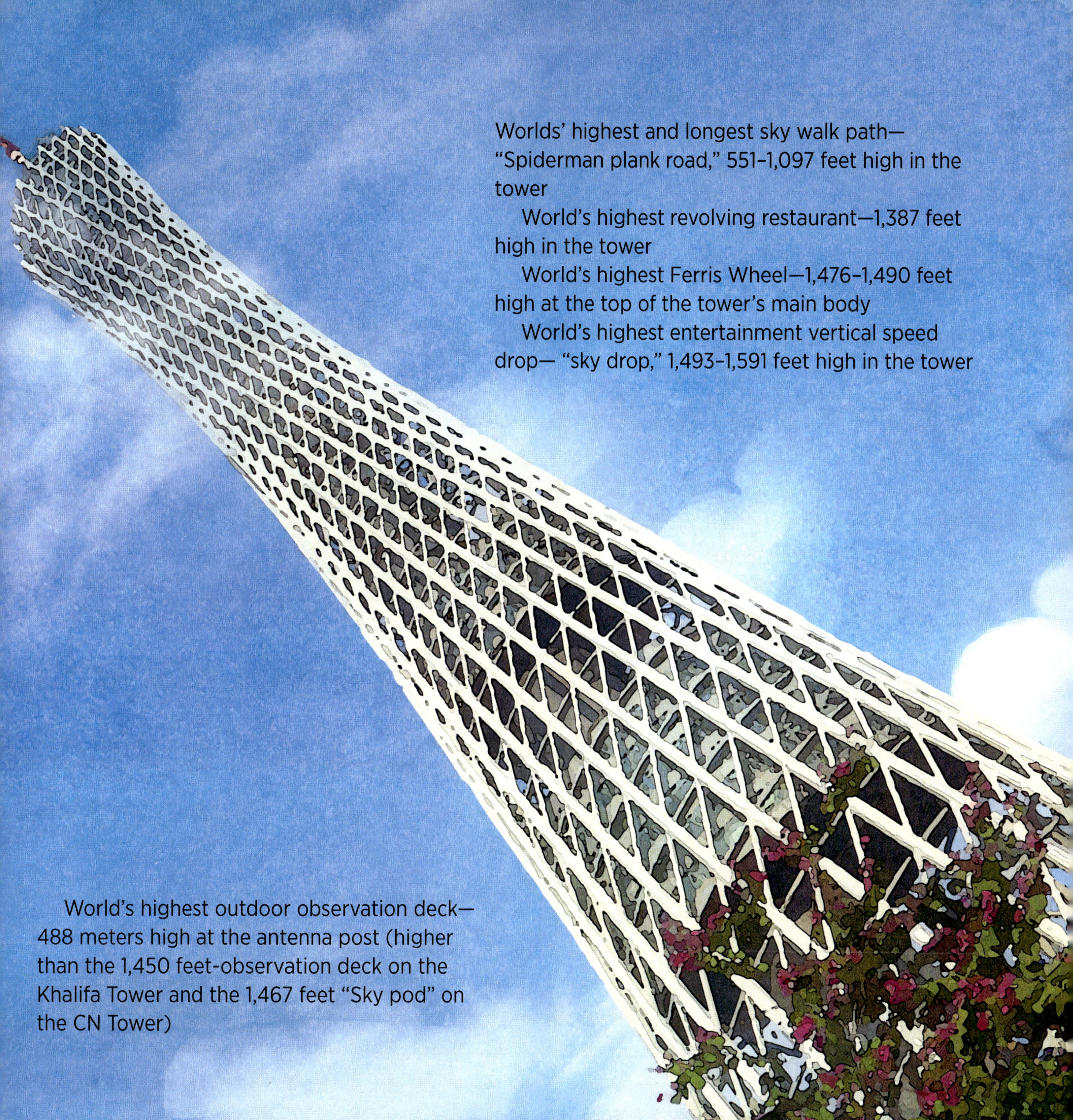

Worlds' highest and longest sky walk path—"Spiderman plank road," 551–1,097 feet high in the tower

World's highest revolving restaurant—1,387 feet high in the tower

World's highest Ferris Wheel—1,476–1,490 feet high at the top of the tower's main body

World's highest entertainment vertical speed drop— "sky drop," 1,493–1,591 feet high in the tower

World's highest outdoor observation deck—488 meters high at the antenna post (higher than the 1,450 feet-observation deck on the Khalifa Tower and the 1,467 feet "Sky pod" on the CN Tower)

Ping An Finance Center of Shenzhen

Height: 1,965 feet, 118 floors
Ranking: tallest building in Shenzhen

Skyscrapers make the peoples' dream of "touching the stars in heaven" a reality.

But people haven't stopped exploring new possibilities. Each year, the eVolo Skyscraper Competition will select the most innovative construction design. Maybe it can give us some ideas of what skyscrapers may look like in the future.

New agriculture community education center and market in the Sahara region

Some people want to change the forests, farmland, and factories into skyscrapers . . .

Some people want to turn skyscrapers into part of nature . . .

A skyscraper built
in the redwoods

Some people think future skyscrapers can be underground, in the water, or in the air . . .

Skyscrapers can not only create more living space for humans but can also provide more services for the society, such as smog control, artificial rainfall, water storage . . .

Air stalactite

Air filters in cities

Water tower in the Himalayas